MISSA
AETERNA CHRISTI MUNERA

FOR

FOUR VOICES

BY

PALESTRINA

EDITED AND ARRANGED FOR MODERN USE BY

HENRY WASHINGTON

———————

Duration of performance 25 minutes

———————

CHESTER MUSIC LIMITED
part of The Music Sales Group
14 -15 Berners Street, London W1T 3LJ, UK

PREFACE

Missa Aeterna Christi Munera takes its title from the Matins hymn for the Common of Apostles. The old proper melody, on which the Mass is based, is nowadays identified— though in restored form—with the Hymn at Terce, *Nunc Sancte nobis Spiritus,* for use on solemn feasts to which no special tune is assigned. Variants of this melody abound. It was known as long ago as the 12th century and may well be of earlier origin. The syllabic version current in the 16th century is printed below for comparison with more familiar forms of the tune* and to show how closely Palestrina follows his chosen *canto fermo.*

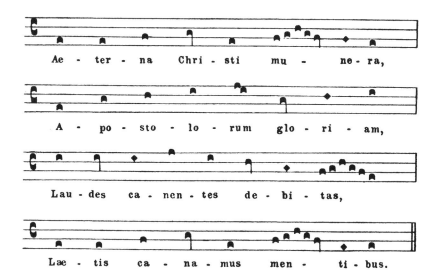

This noble four-line hymn provides three themes which appear in all voices throughout the Mass. One marvels at the subtle transformations which these *motifs* undergo and at the sense of proportion and variety that results from their apt distribution. The first theme serves for *Kyrie 1, Sanctus, Hosanna* and *Agnus Dei* ; the second for *Christe eleison, Dominus Deus Sabaoth* and *Benedictus* ; and the third for *Kyrie 2* and *Pleni sunt coeli.*

A comparatively late work, *Missa Aeterna Christi Munera* expresses Palestrina's art at its simplest and finest. Its ingenious counterpoints are always transparent and it is as easy to listen to as it is to perform. This work, more than any other acknowledged masterpiece of the *Musicae Princeps,* has evoked the admiration of great composers from Bach to Debussy.

The original of this Mass appears in the Liber Quintus Missarum, first published in Rome (1590) and again in Venice (1591). A copy of the 1590 impression is preserved in the British Museum and the present publication has been prepared direct from this source.

* cf. *Antiphonale Monasticum,* 1934, p. 85. The *Liber Usualis,* 1952, p. 235. *Songs of Syon,* p. 261.

Certain practical features of this edition must now be explained. The music text is set out unencumbered with arbitrary marks of expression. Thus, while the choirmaster is at liberty to insert such guides to performance as he thinks expedient, singers are spared the mental conflict induced by his insistence on a *pianissimo* reading when the score demands a contrary effect. The needs of inexperienced choirs have been met by incorporating a suggested scheme of interpretation in the *reductio partiturae*.

The sign ▼, a short vertical stroke placed above or below a note, is freely used in this edition with the two-fold object of defending verbal rhythm against the accentual power associated with the modern bar-line and of defining the true agogic rhythm where an original long note has been replaced by two tied notes of shorter duration. If singers familiar with the Solesmes rhythmic editions of the Chant should confuse this sign with the vertical episema no harm will result, though the sign is here used in a more restricted sense. On the other hand, the usual dynamic signs, bound up as they are with the idea of sudden stress, have been rejected as unsuitable for the purpose.

Missa Aeterna Christi Munera is written in the transposed Ionian mode. It is here reproduced as it stands in the original, a convenient pitch for performance by S.A.T.B. As the voice-lines are set close together the work will nevertheless bear considerable transposition and choirmasters should not hesitate to vary the pitch in accordance with the vocal resources at their disposal. For example, it may be sung a whole tone lower by S.C-T.T.B., a minor third lower by A.T.Bar.B. and even a fourth lower by T.T.B.B.

Original accidentals are printed in the normal position, *i.e.* to the left of the note affected. Other accidentals added by the editor in pursuance of the theory of *musica ficta* appear in small type above the note and are confined for the most part to a naturalizing of B flat under the usual conditions.

The slur is used exclusively to denote a ligature.

Sixteenth-century note-values have been halved to conform to present-day acceptance of the crotchet as the normal unit of time. The quick ternary measure in the Credo at the words *Et in Spiritum Sanctum Dominum* is indicated in the original by the use of black notation.

As to the under-laying of the verbal text, it should be noted that a particular melodic construction often calls for elision of the final E in the words Kyrie and Christe. In such a case the E is printed in italics and is understood to be silent. Kyri*e* eleison is therefore pronounced Kyri' eleison.

For the sake of clarity no attempt has been made to distinguish the original text-indications from the complete distribution of the words undertaken by the present editor. In this task he has been guided by the rules formulated in Palestrina's lifetime by Zarlino and Vicentino. The breathing requirements of average singers have also been taken into account and it is intended that breathing points should be governed by the natural punctuation of the text.

HENRY WASHINGTON.

THE ORATORY,
    LONDON.
        September, 1953.

MISSA AETERNA CHRISTI MUNERA

KYRIE

PALESTRINA
Edited by
HENRY WASHINGTON

GLORIA IN EXCELSIS DEO

SANCTUS

BENEDICTUS

AGNUS DEI I

30

AGNUS DEI II

Soon the music goes out
of print . . . . .

CHESTER MUSIC LIMITED
part of The Music Sales Group
14 -15 Berners Street, London W1T 3LJ, UK

Exclusive distributors:
MUSIC SALES LIMITED
Newmarket Road, Bury St. Edmunds,
Suffolk IP33 3YB, UK